UPSIDE DOWN GRIEF

Divine talks seasoned with grace

Rev Sally Binymin

Sea & Sky

ISBN-13: 9781234567890
ISBN-10: 1477123456

Cover design by: Art Painter
Library of Congress Control Number: 2018675309
Printed in the United States of America

I dedicate this book to my husband Dr K Binymin FRCP;
a giant of generosity, strength and warmth and to
Hannah and Sam. our children who are simply the best!

"I am with you always"

JESUS

CONTENTS

Preface

Loss is too enormous to quantify and no one can measure pain. Grief takes us on a roller coaster ride, often turning up at most inconveneient times. Sometimes our feelings overwhelm us and in those times we may need to be alone to hear the silence in order to help us learn to live within our new reality. Other times, there is room for movement and maybe in those times, one or two of the thoughts contained within these short Christian talks might help to provoke us into a new fold of grace and joy.

Each talk is informal and non academic and written to encourage everyone to keep on being curious about the constancy of love and God's comfort through painful times.

I will never forget you

I will always love you

Thank you for being you

INTRODUCTION

When a random feather arrived in my handbag the first full weekend I spent alone after losing my husband, this really challenged my Christian focus as grief now informed me that comfort may surprisingly arrive in this way. Another feather later appeared on the kitchen floor, filling me with a confidence that under God's wings is my refuge and that grief can be turned upside down. I'm even more confident of this comforting reality as other Christian widows have said similar strengthening moments have happened to them also.

Experiencing such wonder is beautiful and almost a step away from the reality of the tears that flow too often but really we shouldn't be surprised by such revelation or visits from God's angels because we are promised that God will cover us with his feathers and His wings.

So many times we sing about angels in hymns or in more contemporary worship songs but the thought that they may leave their calling card is scandalous and, I admit that at first when it started happening I tried to dismiss it but when it was continuous I had to look up amidst my suffering and give attention to understanding scripture, to understanding life, to understanding God's provision differently to how I had done so previously.

Detaching ourselves from anything that comes to our attention, casts us into the role of observer and then on that basis life can seem even more unreal and just a work of fantasy. The reality therefore lies in our responses to what we see and hear and experience. Sometime ago I

visited an exhibition at the George Pompidou Centre in Paris, where Leandro Erlich created an installation entitled 'le regard'. This is a very comfortable bedroom overlooking the street. From one window is a street in Bombay and from the other a boulevard in Paris. These two worlds are indifferent to each other until they collide, much like when grief and suffering cause a collision, inviting someone extra, someone more mighty than me and you to step into the room, making that world called heaven and our world that we see called earth, so much closer to each other and so much more connected.
Perhaps much of the time we tend to view heaven and earth as separate realities and yet if we live in the Most High's shelter we will rest in the shadow of the Almighty. Psalm 91 showcases such pretty and poetic words, powerful in the midst of grief, anxiety and suffering taking on skin and living its truth through God's embrace bringing stability in such vulnerability , as well as nudging us to keep moving, not outside of the shelter but within His shadow as it moves from day to day.

In His shadow there is a vulnerability that is unique to those who grieve the loss of partners because loneliness cannot be met through people's company as that part of us which made us complete is now missing. We may well be whole people but we have been among those people completed by another. On my own personal journey I choose to live in God's kindly shadow and for me it seems there is a place where joining together still feels possible because the wings that span heaven and earth touch both my husband and myself, as He now rests in the light that creates such shadows here. To rest in this provides a sense of well being and offers comfort. For friends who remain unsure where their relatives have passed to, it is important to remember that when we die we all pass into the hands of God who is love and, it is at the will of His mercy that we are directed into eternity. God made us and to God we return and therefore we can trust God's decisions.

PAINTING THE PICTURE

'I have come that you might have life and have it to the full' #Jesus

Life is like a canvas. When we begin, the canvas is plain and empty but each day builds detail onto the canvas. Grief is overwhelming but in building the canvas, everyday we live and breathe, it is like adding one percent of paint and detail to the painting, because every day is as a small brush stroke. Standing back looking at the canvas, we will all see that some of the space is covered with joyful living, prayer and love but chunks of it are just tear stained and like an ink spillage on the canvas. This suggests a spontaneity that no brush stroke could create alone without the God of full life exploding our view of life and life in all its fullness.

When we consider the miracles encountered by the disciples they were added brush strokes of detail but were not the main focus of the detail, as that lay in the colours of love that merged from relationships of trust, intimacy, respect and love. In using the finer brush strokes God enables us to appreciate the gift of life regardless of imperfections and so we persist in our faith with hope that we will see the glory of God whatever that is, in this!

In living life to its fullest, we experience a whole host of emotions and, at times, we may need to retreat into hiding because the strength of those emotions is too strong or tough for us to bear, or of course we are simply worn out and tired; grief is tiring. That's perfectly acceptable to God who invites us to hide under His wings. In making this journey it has become clear that living life to the maximum isn't about being on the mountaintop but about embracing God and others in whatever we are faced with. When Jesus was in the garden on that fateful night before the crucifixion, He experienced a wealth of emotion that might have given the impression He was tasting less than full life but a closer look reveals that what we witness, is a display of Him being both human and divine. He didn't give up but felt like it. He needed others and knew disappointment when the disciples, his so-called friends, couldn't go the distance with him yet He didn't run away, he embraced the moment. Full life requires guts and it is a choice. However amidst suffering, the design of this full life is a different shape to perhaps what we had expected but whatever shape it is, it is life in all its fullness and for that we are thankful.

ANGELS IN THE WINGS

‘Those who wait on the Lord rise up on eagle's wings’ #Isaiah

Travelling through suffering towards an eternal destiny means waiting. In that wait there is a deepened sense of the Spirit who hovers and lingers around us providing more than a friend in the wait and, amidst our tears we learn to partner with those words ‘not my will but yours Lord’.

The image of rising up on an eagle's wings offers insight into a strength that is beyond normal and suggests that we can expect more than just a laborious and lonely wait. It sounds other and beyond human capacity and it is because along a path of suffering that’s what’s needed. On a path of waiting and suffering Jesus will assign different angels to accompany His travellers and sometimes those people will be human and at other times they will be divine but all are empowered by His Holy Spirit. Jesus promises never to leave us or forsake us and He is always present even in the simplest of exchanges dispatching His angels to meet us and usher us through doors even when they appear closed.

Too often we forget to have conversation with Jesus, and we speak in panicked tones every so often to Him but having a proper chat is something quite different because that involves listening and getting to know our inner spirit. Doing just that introduces us to a wealth of untapped supernatural power within us. The apostle Paul tells us that the Spirit that raised Jesus from the dead is the same Spirit that lives in us and getting to know that Spirit cannot be done through busyness but through waiting and allowing ourselves to be emptied of our agenda, our desire, our passions, even submitting ourselves to death and loss. That sounds too painful and we may feel we should rise with a lion's roar but just because we see the lion's teeth doesn't mean it's smiling! The lion's roar is not about noise, moreover it is a confidence from within that surges with Jesus' power of love to change atmospheres and outcomes.That kind of relationship emerges with a boldness from under His wings when we meet Him who has overcome the powerful sting of death.

ANGELS IN THE VALLEY

'When I walk through the valley, I will not fear because you are with me' #David

Before we can live in a new reality we need to live with angels in the valley where we are led into the realm of impossibilities although, those impossibilities can become possibilities as we bravely walk through the valley. No one stands still, life is an organic journey of movement and of passing through. When Jesus rode towards Jerusalem He kept looking ahead to the changing landscape. Jesus knew He would live beyond death and this is something we too need to embrace as we face our loss. Even though it's quite awful to live without the person whom we may have spent most of our adult life with, it is possible to take daily steps towards tomorrow. When we walk through the valley our moving through is deeply uncomfortable and requires a willingness to let go step by step of the previous step!

Sometimes our view of things is limited by what we know and see. We cannot know that which we cannot know but when Jesus enables our seeing, more becomes possible.

There will be times and God moments each of us can draw upon that will ease the journey, which in turn allows us to see the valley as a holding place where hope can be realised. Being held in the possibility of the belief that no matter what happens in life or death we are always held by the hand that made us, equips us for a next step. The hand who made us is the great artist who uses colours to decorate our lives with ever increasing measures of warmth, all reminding us of His presence. Suffering is not one of those black and white situations but a kaleidoscope of patterns and shades that create shadows of invitation and welcome because wherever we are, God is present.

As God is with us we get to know His shepherd's heart comforting us despite the cruelty of the present loss and separation that creates hesitation and, is that which is among the rips and tears in life that we want to hang onto. That can feel as if life's punctures create the energy and demonstrate the force of gesture that leads to welcome and reconciliation because in brokenness, those things that seemed worth fighting for become less significant. The only thing that seems to matter is faith expressing itself through love. Every grief story is punctuated with dots and commas in the wrong places, but because of those misplaced ellipsis we are nudged into the folds of grace to cope with the sentence of suffering. Shock and grief splinter the soul but angels in the valley remind us that it is with God's help we walk forward to create once again, our own routines which allow us to feel an ordinary sense of participation in the world again. We know we can do it because we have done it before in other situations where our lives were turned upside down. This is just another step and those people we meet or who seem sent alongside us are part of the great cloud of witness. At the time we may not recognise them as angels because our grief is heavy but they are among the people who help us to retain vision and involve us in present hope .

When the shadow of death looms, the valley remains the same but we are changed. As Christians the darkness does not overcome us and God's word brings light and through angels and friends who pray, we begin to slowly see how wonderful it is to be made in God's image.

ANGELS WHO FLY

'When they moved, I heard their wings, it was like the roar of a great waterfall..' #Ezekiel

Moving forward rather than moving on is a better image as we grieve. It somehow feels less harsh. God knows the pain of loss when right from the beginning of time the Eden people separated themselves from following in His direction causing a creative schism that required the intervention of the cross, demonstrating a moving through the chaos and disorder and, on the way establishing blessings that often can only be understood or realised when looking back over the shoulder. Whilst grieving it is difficult to identify blessings and yet in another sense at this time there are so many blessings of love and strength being poured out supernaturally and naturally that they become the trifle that lifts us above our sorrow. Separating that trifle is too complicated and probably it's not even necessary as it is sufficient to trust that God is moving us in the right direction,enabling us to taste hope. Throughout the Bible there is a comforting message that above and beyond all prophecies there is a strength that covers the expanse of heaven and earth and within that we are included and held.

It's super scary cutting through confusion and chaos, which comes with grief, and yet the book of Ezekiel shows through the text, images of humility and power with the seraph and the cherubim spanning more of the earth than we can measure. These images show us the mish mash combination of the divine and human, nature and material mixed together to form a covering over us and, it is clear that these angels are messengers for the glory of God to be

revealed through. None of them acts alone and they work in tandem with one another, empowered by the resting of the cloud of incense upon them, with each continually moving and following the head. Letting go of the loss we feel is needing to say goodbye to so much of who we have been and that isn't comfortable. And, not only do those angels represent movement but in Isaiah it tells us about the wings delivering different functions and one of those functions is to fly, and this presents challenge, especially as we may prefer to rest under the safety of His wings.
As widows/ers missing the strength of a partner, who is now not sharing in decisions, or leading the way in certain circumstances because they are not present to provide an emotional strength and encouragement that has been so helpful over the years, is confronting. In Ezekiel there is a familiarity and recognition of the faces being those the prophet had seen before and from that we may take strength, for who knows what role our partners and other missed relatives now play in the heavenly gallery and, although there is no theological evidence, they may be among those whose wheels keep turning and whose wings rise up and fly. It is an incredible thought to know that the wings that cover us may be some of those we've known and who now attend in the holy of holies and, that is unfathomable.

Those whose hope is in
the Lord will rise.
Never Give Up!

BOOKENDS

'If I climb to the sky, you're there and if I go underground, you're there' # David

Realising that life and death are two bookends but that what counts on earth are the pages in between. Tears and mysterious utterings and groans are useful because they say what we often can't find the words to express. It's through these utterances that joy is manifested and so a sense of knowing that in each day there is so much to be thankful for which powerfully reflects relationships where giving and receiving is paramount, regardless of circumstance. Making a positive choice to find points of gratitude throughout the day lessens the strength of the shadow of death and brings a closeness to God that allows a recentering on His goodness to take place.

Admiring flowers, listening to birdsong and showing gratitude at the sign of a rainbow because it's that picture in the sky that reminds us of something to do with us and God, may sound 'Disney', but it isn't because it's those symbols that make up real everyday life, whether it's a life for a long time or a life for a shorter time on earth .The beauty of relationships, being present in the moment and the endearment of listening to each other from the heart, not just in passing, brings new life. Jesus grabs our attention in the gospels because he isn't speaking endlessly sentence after sentence but He is someone who asks questions and allows us to draw nearer to God through the answer or the discovery of the next challenge He has set us up for.

In living life to the fullest we will experience a whole host of emotion and, at times we may need to retreat into hiding because the strength of that emotion is too strong or tough for us to bear, or of course we are simply worn out and tired. That's perfectly acceptable to God who expects us to hide sometimes under His wings while at other times, we are led to stand tall and shout out aloud on the top of mountains. In some moments we also may cry out in anger toward Him. The psalms show us so clearly how God understands the changing seasons of emotion but let us be assured there is no place that we can go to whether that is emotionally or physically, where He is not there also. His presence is everywhere and nothing will ever seperate us from His love.

You are the apple of God's eye

You are known and loved

You are heard and seen!

UPSIDE DOWN
GRIEF

'I am the resurrection and the life!' #jesus

Smile though your heart is breaking are words from an old song. It's not life if we don't face heartbreak. We meet so many people in life that someone is bound to disappoint us, let us down and even break our heart. We feel a sense of loss in heartbreak and of course the pain of loss cannot be measured.

Loss comes in all shapes but the feelings it evokes bring grief and sorrow. Grief stamps on our heads, stands on our hands and stabs us in the heart. It's painful.

Then, out of the blue something happens to bring about a smile and herein we face a decision. Do we allow that smile to develop and give ourselves the permission to lapse into laughter and, join in with the Spirit or do we turn our backs on allowing ourselves to share in a joyful moment of lighter emotion. It is in those times, despite the sharpness of pain, that it is poignant to allow ourselves this release to relax from the loss and turn grief on its head.

Mary's encounter at the tomb reveals how we can be released from the burden of loss by recognising that death is not the end. Mary came to understand that death is a part of life and that life is a part of death. Jesus overcame death through the power of the resurrection and indeed declared 'I am the resurrection and the life!" and we are reminded in

Paul's letters that if we live to God we will die to Him too. These words are treasures of truthful hope.

Living with such hope and purpose even though we are all dying, some sooner than others, is strengthening. It's strengthening because when we know that God will meet us at every step, we become more God conscious about keeping in step with the Spirit because we cannot do that dance alone. The Spirit of God brings liberty and where the Spirit of the Lord is there is always joy affecting a release in the deep recesses of our being, allowing us to laugh or smile through the brokenness.

However, some people are like professional mourners and they don't allow us to laugh because they project their own grief onto us. Those people place expectations onto us, subliminally forbidding us to smile, or laugh, and they crush hope by using us as their convenient mule for their own losses and pains.

When Jesus arrived at Jairus's house He sent the professional mourners packing, with their absence resulting in a positive response from the dead girl. She woke up. Such an incident is an indication to us that, we too need to be careful whom we allow ourselves to spend time with because we don't want to miss the miracle of life and laughter. Of course people fear being clumsy in their relationship with those who grieve, and saying the wrong thing can cause more pain, but the fragility of relationships is needed because it's that which makes us grow and smile with others and also at ourselves.

Even unto death nothing stays still and we never know how much our own smile will ease another person's pain and, of course, wherever we are on life's spectrum, we still all have meaning. We have the opportunity to express our glad heart which will show as a cheerful face because blessed are those who mourn for they will be comforted, as blessed are the poor in spirit for theirs is the kingdom of heaven.

SECRET STRENGTH

'I am with you always' #jesus

Change is always very challenging but never more challenging than when it arrives uninvited. Adapting to new patterns of living evokes all kinds of emotion because it takes time to allow new habits to develop. There is also the mourning of all that was, that needs to take place but over cooked becomes like burnt toast. When Lazarus died, Martha was angry with Jesus because He didn't do what she had hoped in the time scale she'd planned. It didn't go according to her agenda and she was full of 'if's' So much of our own lives whether we face loss or not, are made up of 'if's' ...If only I had been taller, if only I'd given it more time etc.

Jesus' response to Martha was full of hope but Martha was required to offer an affirmation. In order to access the new circumstance she had to embrace the change and adjust her perspective.

Seeing things differently is necessary in coping with change when living with loss. If we consider how often the shadows in the garden change with the shifting shafts of sunlight, we become privy to the Creator's constancy in change! Our lives, equally created by His design, are no different.

As we navigate the changing times and seasons we see how when the legend Daniel was thrown into the lion's den that he faced immediate loss. Such a plight is likely to cause anger with the resultant attitude of a distancing from God taking place, but Daniel didn't waste energy on misdirected anger, he immediately sought a resolve in God who accompanied him with an angelic presence.

Most people would agree that there are established phases in a process of change that allow precontemplation and contemplation as well as preparation. Yet, when one suddenly lives in the valley of the shadow of death those things aren't available and we are thrown into the action stage where we immediately need to learn a new set of responsibilities, new routines and a new way of being in general. There isn't the choice to return to the way things were but there are new possibilities to challenge ourselves with. Daniel survived the most horrific change where in one minute from being a high ranking civil servant to a second later he became a piece of meat for a lion's dinner. Examples like this encourage us to believe that what Jesus said He meant; I am with you always, even to the ends of the earth' No matter what change besets us, we are not on our own. Daniel's secret strength appeared to be his delight in God even though he faced death...may we all know the same strength to embrace the change as we delight in Him. (But we know some days it's harder than others!)

The One who made you, holds you!

'Do not be afraid' #Jesus

WALKING IN UNCERTAINTY

"How can this be?" # mary

The certainties that once marked off the day are no longer the same and the new pattern overshadows. Most people don't set out in life to waste time doing nothing but when we face loss we realise just how valuable a thing, doing nothing, is because it means we don't need a plan or an agenda, nor do we need a reason to spend time with someone.

Walking in uncertainty is the strategy and means we are freed from being kidnapped or held hostage by our certainties. Those anchors which once held our life secure and sure, are no longer. Opportunities to trust in new ways present themselves in the depths of uncertainty and, waiting in those flickering flames that could become hot or go out at any second, is the new reality.

As children when we travel we ask 'how much longer or how long will it take?' In truth no one can be sure of the journey's time and possibly the answer is, 'it takes as long as it takes'.

Mary through the giving of birth to Jesus was chosen to help fulfil God's plan for humankind and that involved suffering. It was a tough call that involved waiting in different ways throughout the earthly life of her son. She wasn't given the timescale of His life but like any mother, certainly she would have hoped and wanted her son's life to be as long and as full as possible. Mary didn't quit ever, she saw her son abused, rejected, trampled and then crucified. She waited with Him through it all because she was faithful to her promises made that one time, in an uncertain moment in the past, when God surprised her with pregnancy.

When Paul and Peter were in prison, they had no idea what would happen next. They had been beaten, were chained and faced grim circumstances but in the uncertainty of their waiting they sang and praised God which is when the light crept into their cell. An angel shook the foundations and uncertainty was ablaze! Uncertainty invites us to take faith risks and to wait for God.

After Jesus rose again he walked along the Emmaus road with two people. They were chatting on their way, about events of the crucifixion and together they were sharing the loss they felt. Jesus joined them anonymously and they expressed to him their dismay that their hopes were now dashed that he was going to be the one to redeem Israel. Their conversation developed and they explained with amazement that a group of women had reported that he was alive and not dead. Later we discover as Jesus waited with them in their uncertainty that they realised who He was through eating bread, a simple and ordinary act.

Walking in uncertainty clearly reveals newness of relationship, newness of perception, newness of life amidst the loss. Jesus said' dear woman here is your son' Immediately his mother was catapulted into another uncertain relationship with a foster son!

The tension between the certainties of birth and death are those where we walk with God who walks with us. We are not alone!

Sit with me
but
please don't
ask me questions
Stay with me but
please don't
tell me how it was for another
Wait with me
but please don't
try to make me laugh
Be alongside me
and let me cry and
be with me
in the silence,
through the storm,
in the pain
And, in time to come
I will be your angel too.

And this tiredness will pass........

Love lives....on, never dying, even when we say goodbye...

A place we've not seen but our loved ones have is, I imagine, where fresh faces meet, exhultant colours intertwine, exotic flowers perfume the air and where mystery and majesty breathes .

Still, I miss you!

AT A DISTANCE

Where are you Lord?' #David

In dealing with loss there is often anger. Anger in itself is not a negative emotion and can, as we see from Jesus' example, have a positive result in helping us all to rethink our motivation. Jesus turned tables over and made a difference and often anger is the catalyst in moving us forward.

But what about those times when anger and guilt swallow us up because we are disappointed and feel let down. We have to work it out knowing that as long as we dont hurt others in our anger, God is big enough to handle us! God can handle our grief.

David the psalmist asks God where He is and why is He at a distance . He has a general rant at God as he is someone who is troubled and filled with grief. A sense of calm is evident at the closing verses where the psalmist reminds himself of who God is. This is key in dealing with our wounded emotions because so often we look only from where we are standing and we feel weak. But with God who is mighty, there is strength to deal with life because when we feel as though we are in the dark, we can remind ourselves that darkness to God is as light, it just depends on where we are standing!

Finding a sense of normality again is important.It is healthy and necessary for mental wellness to re-introduce ordinariness to the awfulness because in doing so there is a release from living in a fake reality that burdens us with the need to be over protective of ourselves and towards others who suffer.

Words are very powerful and so are our thoughts and sometimes when grief digs her heels in she can create a circular type of thinking that is negative. Corinthians tells us to take captive our thoughts because if we allow negative thoughts to develop we will allow the negative committee too much of a voice.

Praying for others even when we hurt allows God to take us beyond the surface of things and to lead us to a place where conventional meaning and perceptions of reality move, breathe, vibrate and break open a new beginning where friendships may emerge. It's when this kind of thing happens that life for us all begins to be re-worked and re-directed in the light of the infinite possibilities of God's love.

AFTER DEATH

'He is the image of the invisible God and in Him all things hold together' #Paul

Miracles still happen in all kinds of shapes, forms and sizes as God is displaying His love through each of us as we become the movers and shakers in His continuing pursuit of healing and wholeness .It's vital that we continue to ask for miracles and believe that God is able to do more than we ask for. Miracles aren't always healings but they are acts of God which point to His glory. To receive more of Him, more power, more love, more of His greatness, is a miracle. We can encourage each other to seek God for a miracle, just a miracle. It's so tempting to give a long list of what we think the miracle will be or should be but there is something extraordinary that happens within ourselves and sometimes around us, when we simply ask in the name of Jesus, for a miracle.

Miracles are those moments that fill us with gratitude because they are unexpected encounters, unexpected touches, unexpected realisations that God is on our side and His best intention for us all is in the centre of His heart. If God is for us, who can be against us!

Too often we see things from our perspective or through our limitations and inabilities but God has another way of seeing. We cannot compare ourselves to God. Indeed we have not measured the waters in the hollow of our hand nor held the dust of the earth in a basket and at the drop of a hat we become tired and weary. But those who wait upon the Lord will renew their strength and will soar on wings like eagles! In other words when the stuffing is knocked out of us, we will rise again!

Having an informed image of God is key in receiving and, in Colossians we are reminded that Christ is the image of the invisible God and that in Him all things hold together! To know that, is in itself a miracle and in knowing this, it further informs us more about the permanent metamorphosis of the world we see and reminds us too, that the image of God in others is an endless mutual reflection of constancy and stillness, creativity and kindness in which we recognise Christ, the invisible.

Jesus is the word of life and that's why living in the Word, reading the Bible is paramount for miracles to happen. The Word releases into us an enigmatic miracle that we actually don't need to understand nor do we need to undermine its power because we can't quantify it beyond knowing it did something… and when we look back we see that it was a miracle!

'Come to me all you who are weary and burdened and I will give you rest. Take my yoke upon you for my burden is light and my yoke is easy' #jesus

These are very powerful words that have at their heart our very best interest. When the weight of loss and grief are too much, remembering these invitational words from God, our host, offers relief and comfort.

Coming to Jesus requires something extra to occur behind the scenes in our attitude because unless we know our need and our inability to create resolve for ourselves , then we will always remain at a distance. Two people can share the same space but if there is no connection they are distant. God doesn't need to get on a plane or travel miles to meet us, His Spirit is with us but until we plug in we will not be charged with His energy.

In coming to Jesus over and over again through different states and situations it becomes apparent that a life of prayer is like bite sized scenes of a film being played out in eternity although of course, this life that we live is no work of fiction and there are no dress rehearsals. Yet if we stand back passively and don't come to Jesus in prayer we are neglecting the one conversation that joins us into being a participant partner in God's mission. When Jesus died the curtain of the temple was torn in two giving us a clear view of a world that God cares intimately about. There is no indifference with God whose mission is to heal the heart of the world. The resurrection of Jesus, challenges us to live beyond the window's reflection, knowing that the pain, destruction and fear we see and experience is not a riot that God created, yet he waits for us to respond so that through us He may once again display His hands of love and heart of kindness, not with a wave through the window but with pure heartfelt participation in prayerful action.

Involving Christ in every season of our life and along the way of suffering helps us to know God did not put us in the valley. The valley is a passageway in life that at different times we pass through. That is life. Why me is not a response to our circumstances because we can equally say 'why not me?'

We all have the invitation to 'Come to Him'because God doesn't have favourites although at times in specific ways He may show favour to accomplish His purpose!

When we come to Jesus in the valley or in the shadowy times, it's often to nag Him to get us out of this or that or, to move us on or to sort out the difficulty we face. But there is a place to be still and to allow His love to embrace us in a way that we may not experience or understand fully when the sun shines. Getting to know Christ in times of adversity releases us from some of those dominating structures we've been subject to or activity protocols that have overshadowed our relationship with God. This is a different season, where those rules and regulations don't work anymore because now the focus is our relationship and in grief we need to learn the art of being in the presence of God.

Come to me and come up higher God says because deep calls to deep and in the valley we have time to go deeper rather than treating the valley within a trauma response. There is so much more to receive than we have already seen, heard and touched. Coming to God with open hands and open hearts and a willingness to allow God to work through us, makes His heart melt because this valley is full of others too, and with our hearts beating to the rhythm of mission we never lose hope or purpose in our determination and desire to please God.

A CLOUDY EXPERIENCE

'A day is like a thousand years and a thousand years is like a day' #Peter

It's been said that in order to stand up strong we need to have first knelt down. In the shadowy times it's easier to fall foul to adopting the persona of a victim and then the love mantle that God placed on us becomes less effective. Certainly being caught up in our own suffering, and immersed in our own awfulness means we forget about other people's needs and in doing so, really we also stop loving ourselves. However, it takes energy and determination to shift our gaze yet when we do, beauty envelops us in the most unexpected of ways. That beauty seems to arise from smoked ashes because under all that trauma and unpredictability is a constant beckon, a constant pursuit of reconciliation where God is drawing us by His Spirit and enigmatically so, by whatever means.

Whoever we are and whatever we have it is not ours and we are not our own because we belong to Christ, bought by His blood. That sounds slightly crazy because when we are about to lose everything surely we tighten our grip on the little we have left. That may be the case at times but when the Spirit speaks to us in those quieter, more still moments, there seems to emerge a willingness to agree that actually being wrapped in a label that shouts CHOSEN is a greater comfort than anything material and explainable. We are of course part of a great cloud of witness and throughout a journey of suffering it may encourage us to look up at the clouds that ceaselessly drift with abstract patterns painting the sky all bringing us closer to God as He delights in our gratitude .As part of a great cloud of witness we are reminded of the work of Louise Bourgeois, a sculptor whose work focused on themes of human expression. She considered her abstract works to be narratives of emotion and wanted them to convey some sort of human condition that language alone could not fully communicate. One of her sculptures depicted clouds and this, for her, revealed the calming effect of repetition. Obviously when we are upset or weighed down and face a crisis, the power of written and traditional prayer can ease our struggle and something familiar like the Lord's Prayer is helpful to remind us of who God is. In those times such prayers work well as they provide a structure in chaos and a reminder of a God who provides. The Lord's Prayer is a prayer that says so much and gives us a pattern to live by. Eventually,the repeated prayer lifts us above our sorrow and chaos to focus our attention on praise. Praising God for who He is, giving thanks and proclaiming hallelujahs over ourselves and others, shifts atmospheres.

On this grief journey, Jesus has created within us, a hopeful curiosity and although as Christians we are called to a life of prayer and watching, those prayers tend to change because curiosity allows us to step inside a world of love which may not previously have been visited. That's not to suggest we haven't loved before or spoken good words over others but amidst our pain, love takes a new shape that is less about the limitations, or the boundaries and more about the centre that just grows to include more and more of our wobbly humanity. Discovering a door that opens to limitlessly bless others is liberating and removes urgency, making time a gift for us to spend joyfully loving each other here on earth.. No one knows the time when the Lord will return but to be an active prayer partner with the Spirit of God and others, is to live life to the full, regardless of circumstance. There is a sense about what happens today, what happens now, in this moment, being vitally important but once it's gone, it's gone and to chase it, is to miss the 'now' moment that, curiously with hope, draws us forward.

To live in the light of suffering gives us entrance to meet hope and joy in a very different way. In meeting hope through our pain is an unfolding of sharing in God's DNA . Knowing Christ by sharing in His sufferings deepens our gratitude because Christ's Spirit is here and is an ever present help. There is a tangible closeness that cannot be explained away .

He holds our hand to help Him accomplish on earth His heavenly will. That's exciting because despite the struggle and adversity, we are useful in a plan that is so much bigger than our mind can ever understand. Standing on Christ's shoulders there are only solutions with generosity and kindness and, above all, love.

Through grief we learn the power and importance of not just prayer but of God's word because it is the Word that became life and lived amongst us and still lives with us by His Spirit.

We may not feel like emotionally standing and walking but we are called to do so and as we keep in step with the Spirit, we will be enabled but we must make sure we eat plenty so that we are not weakened. Eating plenty for Christians is dining on the Word of God and worshipping and, as we hold onto the Word of God, so God holds onto us!

TICK TOCK

'Though I don't see the fig tree bud and there are no grapes on the vine and there are no sheep in the pen or cattle in the stalls, I will still rejoice..'
Habakuk

Clock hands tick with time changing by an hour marking the winter and summer seasons and, in between we all enjoy the gift that time allows. How we use our time is something we learn to manage from being a small baby. We learn what time means through feeding patterns and having our needs met by our caregivers. As we move through life time presents itself through many different faces but in dying, time teaches us to live well.

Knowing that God created time means that in time we will meet each other again and that our passing through this life is part of the time apportioned to us in helping to steward the earth, enabling us to contribute towards building God's kingdom in the here and now.

So often we pray hoping to see something happen at a certain time but a different answer besets us, much like Habakuk's experience but because the prophet knew the strength of God in a time of crisis, he was able to trust God.

Habakkuk was confident in God whom he said owned the cattle on a thousand hills, declaring also that God would make his feet swift like a deer to run and rise to the heights.

Time for Habakuk was of the essence but for God it was just something that was perfect when it was in step with the Spirit's timing.

Accepting that God has an ordained number of days for each of us to live is not something we can do without the presence of His love enabling and empowering us towards an acceptance that this is part of those words we so often say,'thy will be done on earth as it is in heaven'. Recognising that death is as beautiful and as meaningful as life, is a realisation that equips us to make daily decisions about some of the things that we need to allow to die or to let go of. We live in a culture where we feel we need to do things to death to get our money's worth or to accrue the investment of time we've made. Allowing things in our lives to die is always sweet when at a later time we see a new something springing up or growing in its place.

Yet renewal on earth for our bodies is not necessarily something we can expect in our lifetime and so we console ourselves that we are all offered the gift of time to love God, and to love our neighbour as ourselves. For some, that may mean seeking forgiveness, for others it may involve offering a reconciling hand but for all it's an equal opportunity to chase God with passion and to find the friendship Moses had when God spoke with him face to face. Time allows us to invite the lamp of our first love to burn again because His eyes are on us and, never more than when we give Jesus our time!

EPILOGUE

There is life after death which means we can face tomorrow and, I thank God that it is possible to smile again. Pain and loss and grief are not those who influence me because I have come to understand that although they maybe present, it is only Jesus who has power! His power is love.

AFTERWORD

In an upside down journey of grief, suffering and loss create an embrace of a valley experience, causing a closer look at Jesus' words about life in all its fullness. The journey provides no answers, creates questions and is as joyful as it's sad. It's upside down when we laugh and share joy in God's goodness and hope.

FINAL THANKS

Thank you Jesus for moving in and keeping me company everday!

ACKNOWLEDGEMENT

Many thanks to Brenda and Felicity who in this first year of loss have helped me to keep moving but who have also stood still with me when needed.

Thanks to all my praying friends too; with your continued prayers and love, I know I am strengthened.

ABOUT THE AUTHOR

Rev Sally Binymin

Sally is a retired Methodist Minister who prior to entering the church worked as a social worker after being educated at Southampton University.
She worked freelance broadcasting for Radio 4's religous programmes and local radio. She has also contributed to programmes such as Blue Peter and written regularly for Scripture Union Magazines.
Sally is mum to Hannah and Sam and was together with her husband for 30 years. Her dog Pickle helps her meet new friends in her neighbourhood!

PRAISE FOR AUTHOR

'Treasures of truthful hope; offering an honest reflection of how grief and faith intertwine'
Rev Steve Swann Methodist Church

'A poignant and moving look at grief and how it affects us ; a book that helps us to move forward'
Rev Malcolm Dyer Elim Church

'Sally captures how to walk through the valley with Jesus and friends; moving & real'
Rev Marilyn Harry Love Wales

Printed in Great Britain
by Amazon

47083803R00046